BORN TODAY, BORN YESTERDAY: REINCARNATION

BY GWEN RISEDORF

A

cpi

Book

From

RAINTREE CHILDRENS BOOKS
Milwaukee • Toronto • Melbourne • London

Library of Congress Number: 77-21406

Art and Photo Credits

Cover illustration by Lynn Sweat.
Illustrations on pages 7, 15, 17, 23, 27, 29, 33, 36, 45, and 47, Jeffrey Gatrall.
Photos on pages 9, 10, 22, and 39, Wide World Photos.
Photo on page 19, The Granger Collection.
Photo on page 24, Pictorial Parade, Inc.
Photo on page 41, Mockingbird Press.
All photo research for this book was provided by Sherry Olan and Roberta Guerette.
Every effort has been made to trace the ownership of all copyrighted material in this
book and to obtain permission for its use.

Library of Congress Cataloging in Publication Data

Risedorf, Gwendolyn, 1923-
   Born today, born yesterday: reincarnation.
   SUMMARY: Briefly investigates the possibility of reincarnation by
presenting accounts of people who claim remembrances from past
lives.
   1. Reincarnation—Juvenile literature. [1. Reincarnation] I. Title.
BL515.R57   236   77-21406
ISBN 0-8172-1045-8 lib. bdg.

Manufactured in the United States of America.
ISBN 0-8172-1045-8

CONTENTS

THE STRANGE CASE OF BRIDEY MURPHY

One evening in 1952, a young housewife who lived in Colorado agreed to take part in an hypnosis experiment. She would be put in a *trance*, or deep sleeplike state. The man who hypnotized her was Morey Bernstein. The young woman's name was Ruth Simmons.

After putting Mrs. Simmons into a trance, Bernstein began his questioning. Little by little, he led Mrs. Simmons back into her childhood. He asked her to try to remember what her life had been like—at 15, at 8, at 5. Eventually, she reached back to the age of one year. She could even remember certain toys she had loved as a child. With such a willing subject at hand, Bernstein decided to conduct another session.

"Ruth," he said to her at the beginning of their second session, "this time we are going to take you back even farther. Hopefully, you will go beyond the childhood you know as your own and find yourself in some other scene, in some other place, in some other time. You will be able to talk to me about it and answer my questions." She nodded sleepily as she went deeper and deeper into the trance.

After a few moments, Bernstein said softly, "Now, Ruth, I want you to go back to the time before you were born and tell me what you see."

The voice that answered Bernstein was that of a little girl with an Irish accent. "I live in Cork [Ireland]," she said. "My name is Bridey Murphy. It is the year 1806. My father is a barrister [lawyer] named Duncan. My mother's name is Kathleen. I have one brother. I later married Brian MacCarthy and we went to live in Belfast."

Bernstein was shocked. Was he really hearing the voice of another person? Did this person really live in 1806, in Cork, Ireland? More shocking—was this Ruth Simmons once someone called Bridey Murphy? As the session continued, "Bridey Murphy" told of other incidents in that long ago lifetime. She told Bernstein that after her death, she had lived in the spirit world for 40 years. She was then born again in Iowa, in 1923—as Ruth Simmons.

Born again? Is it really possible for a person to have once lived a completely different life? Those who believe in *reincarnation* think it is. They say that a person born today could also have been born in some other yesterday.

When the story of "Bridey Murphy" hit the newspapers, people were shocked. The very idea of reincarnation was hard to believe. Many writers, scientists, and reporters felt that it was all a hoax. Morey Bernstein and Ruth Simmons were playing a great trick on the public.

A team of investigators from *Life* magazine set out to find Ruth Simmons in her Iowa hometown. When they arrived there, the reporters learned that there were many Irish people who lived near Ruth Simmons. Many of

Morey Bernstein shows "Ruth Simmons" mail he receives concerning Bridey Murphy.

them were her friends and neighbors. She could easily have picked up all details of life in Ireland from them. The investigators concluded that this was how Ruth Simmons came to believe she was Bridey Murphy.

But the story did not end there. A reporter from the *Denver Post* refused to accept *Life* magazine's interpretation of the strange case. He decided to go to Cork, Ireland, for himself, to check out Ruth Simmons' story.

The reporter returned with astounding news. No matter how much her Irish neighbors knew about Cork, they could not have given Ruth Simmons all of the details she had known

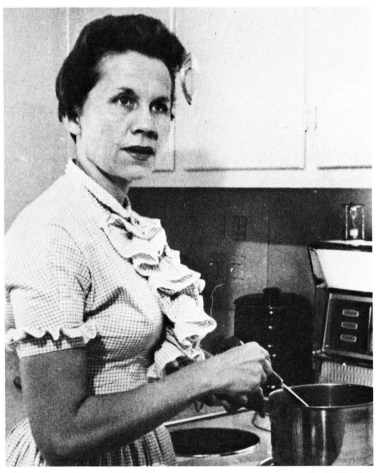

To protect her real identity, the young woman was called "Ruth Simmons" at the time of the Bridey Murphy story. Really Virginia Tighe, she lives simply, as a housewife.

about Bridey. Ruth Simmons could not have known so much about the Bridey Murphy in Cork unless she really *was* Bridey Murphy.

Today, Mrs. Simmons lives a quiet life in Arizona. In her normal conscious state, when she is not in an hypnotic trance, she cannot remember ever having been "Bridey Murphy."

But the question of Bridey Murphy still rages on. Scientists believe that reincarnation just can't be proved one way or the other. Are these memories of other lives true or false? Let's see what reincarnation really means.

TRAPPED INSIDE A NEW LIFE

Do you think you have ever lived at another time, in another body? Is it possible to lead two, three, even four different lives? From the beginning of time, people have asked themselves these questions. They are seeking the answer to reincarnation, the belief that a human being can return from death to live a new life.

Reincarnation means "born again." The ancient Greeks and Egyptians believed that when a person died, only the body's life was over. The soul, or spirit of that person, lived on. Eventually, the soul finds its way into the body of another living thing—a human, an animal, a bird, even a flower.

Later civilizations believed that the soul returned to earth in a very special way. If the person lived like an animal, he or she would become an animal in the new life. But if the person lived a good life, he or she would be reborn as a human being. Some believe that the new life often depends on what the old life was like. The poor might become rich in the new life if they had been good in the old life. The beautiful could return as ugly people as a punishment for their bad deeds in the old life.

Most important, the new life would not be the last. The person could continue to be reincarnated in countless lifetimes.

The idea of reincarnation has been explored scientifically only in recent years. But long before that, people had questions and ideas about reincarnation. In the *Koran,* the holy book of the Islamic religion, it says: "God generates beings and sends them back over and over again, till they return to Him." And the *Druses,* a religious group that practiced their beliefs during the eleventh century, described a remarkable tale of reincarnation.

A child of five, living in Djebel el A'ala (an ancient town in Syria), complained about the horrible life of poverty his parents led. The boy claimed that once, in another life, he had been a rich man in Damascus (another town in Syria). The little boy said that when he died, he was born in another place where he lived for only six months.

After that brief life, the boy was born again into his present life of poverty in Djebel el A'ala. But the child was very unhappy. He wanted to go back to his old hometown, the one from two lives before.

Finally, the boy's family agreed to take him to Damascus for a visit. On the way, they were in for their first big surprise. Their son knew all the names of the different places they passed —even though he had never traveled that route before! But that was only the beginning.

When they finally reached Damascus, the boy led the way through the various streets to a house. The child claimed that this house had been where he lived—in his *first* life.

The child knocked on the door. When the owner of the house answered, he called her by

To the woman's surprise, the boy at the door
greeted her by name.

her name. Again the boy's family was shocked.
How did he know the strange woman's name?
When the woman let him in the house, the boy
said that he had once been her husband. He
even asked after the welfare of *their* several
children. The woman could not believe what
she was hearing. She became very frightened.

The Druses of Damascus soon heard of
this strange young boy. They came to the

house to see if there was any truth in this mysterious story. The child gave them a full report of his past life in Damascus. He told them the names of his former friends and about the land he had once owned. Several people investigated the young child's story. Everything he had told them so far was true.

Only one fact had not been checked. The boy told of a small sum of money which he said a certain weaver had owed him before he died. The Druses sent for the weaver and asked about the money. At first the weaver was frightened. Finally, he confessed, "Yes, it is true. I did owe him money, but I was too poor to pay it back to his children after he died."

The child then asked "his wife" if she had found the money he had hidden in the cellar. She hadn't. The boy led her to the cellar himself and began digging in a particular spot. Soon he uncovered a dusty sack. Inside was the money he had hidden in his "other" life.

Did the child really live three lives? Was he once a rich man in Damascus? It's impossible to know for sure. But many people since that time have had similar experiences.

He dug up a cloth sack which had been buried in the dirt floor.

3

OTHER TIMES, OTHER PLACES

One stormy February night in 1828, Sir Walter Scott, a British novelist, sat in his bedroom. He was thinking about what to write in his diary for that day. Outside, the bare tree limbs scratched against his window pane. A candle flickered on his desk casting shadows on the wall. And the last of the embers in the fireplace made tiny sighs as they burned to ashes.

Picking up his pen, Sir Walter began writing. "I cannot, I am sure, tell if it is worth mark-

Sir Walter Scott, the famous British author, felt that the things that were happening he had experienced before.

ing down. But at dinner time I was strangely haunted by what I could call a sense of pre-existence [having lived before]. It was an idea that nothing that passed was said for the first time. That the same things we talked about we had talked about before. The same people, saying the same things. The sensation was so strong it was what might be called a mirage [an illusion] in the desert. It was very distressing, with a sense of unreality in all I said or did."

Memories of reincarnation come to people at different times in their lives, often when they least expect them. Some people have dreams that hint of other lives. A person might see herself doing things or being in places that are totally unknown to her in her waking life. Others, like Bridey Murphy, get in touch with their past through hypnosis. And sometimes, as in Sir Walter Scott's case, people get strange "flashes" when they're awake. These experiences, called *déjà-vu* (French for "already seen"), are often related to reincarnation memories. And they're often very frightening experiences.

Another writer described his *déjà vu* this way: "At sunset, when I was walking alone, while the horses rested, I came upon a place which, though I had never been there before, was instantly familiar to me. I see it clearly now.

"In the foreground is a group of silent peasant girls, leaning over the side of a little bridge. In the distance there is a deep valley. The shadow of approaching night crept up on everything. If I had been murdered there in some former life, I could not have seemed to remember the place more thoroughly or with more frightening chilling of the blood. Although I cannot say for sure it ever happened, I hardly think I could ever forget it."

And a German *physicist* (a scientist who studies matter and energy) wrote, "I cannot get rid of the thought that I died before I was born. I feel so many things that, were I to write them down, the world would regard me as a madman."

When Charles Lindbergh made his historic flight across the Atlantic Ocean, he flew alone, day and night, for 34 hours. During that long flight, he described what happened:

"The fuselage [the space behind the engine where he sat] became crowded with ghostly human presences, transparent, riding weightless within the plane. I felt no surprise in their being there. I discovered I did not even have to turn my head to see them all at the same time, for it seemed my skull had become one great eye, seeing everywhere at once."

Captain Charles Lindbergh, a former air mail pilot, with the Spirit of St. Louis, before his historic flight to Paris in 1927.

As the flight continued, Lindbergh was troubled by his "passengers": "The spirits seemed to be able to appear or disappear whenever they chose, passing through the walls of the plane as though no walls existed. I heard familiar voices in the plane advising me, encouraging me, and giving me instructions, as though I've known all of them before in some past incarnation [life]."

Lindbergh felt the plane was filled with ghosts, advising and encouraging him during his flight.

Who had climbed aboard the plane? Was Lindbergh overtired from his long, lonely flight? Or were there other "humans" with Lindbergh? Were they the souls of people who once lived —souls that would eventually find their way into other bodies?

For some people, reincarnation is neither strange nor frightening. To them it's a comforting thought to know that the soul lives on through the ages. Jack London, a famous writer of adventure tales, was one person who seemed to like the idea of being reborn.

An informal portrait of writer Jack London, taken in 1916.

In his fictional story, "The Star Rover," London tells of a prisoner. Though the man's body is trapped in a straight jacket, he still feels that his spirit is free: "All my life I have had an awareness of other times and places. I have been aware of other persons in me . . . I remember that I had once been the son of a king. More, I remember that once I had been a slave and had worn an iron collar around my neck. All of my previous selves have their voices and echos prompting me. And I shall be born again. . . ."

4

THE REMARKABLE EDGAR CAYCE

Nine-year-old Edgar was a disgrace to his father, Squire Cayce. In school that day, the boy had failed to spell a simple word—"cabin." Angry and determined to sharpen the boy's mind, Squire Cayce reviewed the day's schoolwork with Edgar. And when his patience wore thin, the Squire boxed his son until the boy fell off his chair.

Suddenly, as he lay on the floor, young Edgar heard voices: "If you can sleep a little, we can help you." Edgar had no idea where the voices came from. But he listened to them.

"Father," asked Edgar, "would it be all right if I rested for a few minutes?"

Squire Cayce agreed, but he warned Edgar that the lesson was not over. And when he returned from the kitchen, Edgar had better know his words.

Fifteen minutes later Mr. Cayce returned to find his son asleep. Instead of studying his spelling book, the boy was using it as a pillow! Now

Young Edgar removed his pillow, and went to sleep with the book under his head.

more furious than ever, he awoke Edgar by pulling the book from under his head.

"Wait!" cried the boy, still a little drowsy from his short nap. "I know my words now." The father listened in disbelief as Edgar recited his lessons. Thinking his son had been pretending all along, he spanked the boy again and sent him to bed.

Edgar didn't care too much about being sent to bed. After all, he had just discovered an amazing talent. Despite his father's suspicions, Edgar hadn't been trying to fool him. He now knew that all he had to do was sleep on a book—then he could repeat its contents word for word! From then on, he was one of the best students in school.

For Edgar Cayce it was only the first of many unbelievable discoveries. And it wasn't long before the other people in the small town where he lived realized Edgar was a most unusual person.

Edgar Cayce was born in 1877 and died in 1945. When he was 21 years old, Edgar realized he could "tune in" to other people's minds and bodies. Merely by using his mind Edgar could

When Cayce put himself in a trance he could look into the past and see former lives.

"examine" people. He could describe an illness —and even tell the person what to do about it! This was very strange because Edgar Cayce was no doctor. He had never studied medicine. In fact, he had never gone past the seventh grade!

In his waking life Edgar Cayce was a children's photographer. Yet, when he lay down on the sofa and put himself in a trance, he knew as much about the human body as any trained doctor. The word of his remarkable gift that could cure the ill soon spread.

Cayce seemed to "see" things in his trances —things he could not possibly know. People would come to him to solve their health problems, see their future, tell them what to do to get well. When someone asked for a *reading*, as these "tuning ins" were called, Edgar would lie down on a couch. He would breathe deeply for a few seconds and then fall into a trance. Unlike most people, Edgar needed no hypnotist to put him in this sleeplike state. He could do it himself.

For many years Edgar Cayce used his remarkable powers only to examine people's physical conditions and to help heal them. But in later years, his readings took a new turn. Edgar discovered that he could also use his talents to look into the past and see the other lives people had once lived. In doing these *life readings*, Edgar could find out the reasons for people's behavior in their present lives. One of his earliest life readings was his own.

CAYCE'S LIFE READINGS

In doing life readings on himself, Edgar Cayce found out the reason for his own powers and why he was such a good healer. Cayce learned that he had once been a high priest in ancient Egypt. And in that life, he was also different from other people. He had great magical powers that enabled him to see into the future.

Cayce was then reincarnated as an Arabian chief. In this second lifetime, he experienced great pain and bodily torture. Fortunately, that life was short.

Next, Cayce discovered, he lived in Persia as a physician. He built a large healing center where people could come for diets, herbal medicines, and steam baths. Obviously, his interest in medicine had continued into his next life, the one that had begun in 1877, when he was "reborn" in Hopkinsville, Kentucky.

When Edgar Cayce first discovered this ability to give life readings, it frightened him a little. He wasn't even sure he believed in reincarnation. But as time went on, Cayce changed his views. Time and time again, the "facts" he found in his life readings proved true. Cayce was able to describe long ago times in history with incredible accuracy. He told of events, people, and places that he had no way of knowing about. And through this knowledge of the past, Cayce could help people understand more about their lives in the present.

Some people asked Cayce for life readings so they could decide what job they were best suited for. By understanding what they had done best—or worst—in other lives, it gave them clues for the present. Once, Edgar Cayce told a young woman that she was wasting her time as a telegraph operator. Her true talents were in art. She had never considered an art ca-

In other lives, Cayce believed he had been an Egyptian priest, an Arabian chief and a Persian doctor.

reer, nor had she any training in the field. But she decided to take a chance. To her surprise, she was an extremely talented student who went on to become a very successful artist.

Sometimes troubled parents brought a child to Edgar Cayce. They couldn't understand the child's behavior. And they hoped a life reading would shed new light on their problem.

One mother was worried about the way her son was acting. She just couldn't seem to get along with the boy. He seemed to resent his mother. And he would not obey any of her instructions. Hearing of Cayce's power to "tune in" to the lives of children, the anxious woman brought her child to Cayce's house for a reading.

Once in a trance, Cayce spoke to the worried parent. "In his previous life this soul was a gold miner in California. But he became disgusted with the lawlessness and violence of that period in history. In time, he was stripped of all his earnings and eventually died a violent death. Because of that, this soul is terribly frightened of guns. These weapons should never be allowed in his presence. Such explosions are frightening to this soul."

Pausing again—it was as though he was reading from an imaginary book—Cayce continued. He was making further contact with the soul of the little boy.

"He will always seek new fields of activity, for everything about this soul must be new. It won't be easy for you to keep up with him. In fact, don't be surprised if he tells you you're out of date!"

Curious to know more about the "other lives" her son had led, the boy's mother brought him to Cayce for several life readings. To say the least, she was shocked to learn that her son may have led other lives in the past.

"This soul was once an important person in Roman times. He was a rich man who was in charge of collecting taxes. When the ancient continent Atlantis sank beneath the sea, he helped many people find their way to new homes in Egypt."

The boy's mother and father both accompanied him to the last reading. Cayce told them that they had been with the boy in his former life. When their son had been in the California gold fields, his father had been with him then, too. In fact, the boy's father wasn't a father at all in *that* life. He was his son's good friend.

As always, Cayce's slender, rather frail body was stretched out on the couch. He closed his eyes, breathed deeply for a few seconds, then lapsed into his sleeping state. His secretary was always in the room to write down everything that was said while he gave his readings.

"You and your son were old friends in California," Cayce told the boy's father. "And before that, you were both together in Egypt at

Cayce told the
surprised family
of their son's
previous lives.

the time of the Exodus. His mother was there, too, but then she was not your son's mother. Because the three of you have been together so many times in the past—in different relationships—there will be times in the present relationship when your son will doubt your authority."

Imagine the surprise the parents felt to hear that all three of them had lived other lives together in Rome and Egypt. More astounding—they all returned to a new life together once again!

How much of this is true? No one knows. Reincarnation cannot be studied under a microscope. Although many of his readings *have* been proven true, scientists do not say Cayce's work proves that reincarnation does happen. But many are still trying to find out.

Cayce gave approximately 2,500 life readings between 1923 and 1945, when he died. And he left behind an extraordinary mass of information—notes on all his cases and research that back up his visions. Perhaps someday the work of Edgar Cayce will help solve the mystery of reincarnation after all.

TRACKING DOWN THE TRUTH

6

Does reincarnation really occur? Is there a link between past and present lives? Can people really return from the past to live in the present? Will these same people live again and again in the future? Nobody knows the answers. But there are people investigating this strange phenomenon right now.

At Duke University in North Carolina, scientists are searching for keys to unlock the mystery of reincarnation. Dr. J. B. Rhine, an expert on the subject at Duke, says, "We have collected thousands of incidents, several hundred of which seem to indicate that the teller of the

At Duke University, Dr. J. B. Rhine heads the Parapsychology Laboratory, which looks into the mysteries of reincarnation and other unexplained happenings.

tale believes as truth what has happened to him. . . ."

So far, the only "evidence" of reincarnation comes from people who believe they've lived before. It's not much to work with, but scientists have no choice. When a person reports a reincarnation dream or a strange *déjà vu*, the experts often use hypnosis to check the story. They put the person in a trance and ask them to reveal information about other lives. Notes are taken. Then researchers try to track down evidence that would support—or disprove—the person's "other-life" story.

As time goes by, more people like Edgar Cayce—called *psychics* or *clairvoyants*—will be called on to work with these scientists who are researching reincarnation. Unfortunately, because scientists were not very interested in the subject during Cayce's lifetime, he never had this chance. Therefore, most of his cases are not recognized by the experts. In Cayce's day, there were no trained psychic investigators as there are today. There was no careful follow-up of his subjects' lives. And no scientist actually sat in on his readings. Hopefully, another person with Edgar Cayce's gifts will come along again. This time he or she probably won't be ignored.

Other clues to the mysteries of reincarnation have come from people who have *almost* died. They have been pronounced dead and then revived. Or they have suffered severe illness or injuries that brought them near death. Raymond Moody is a doctor who is interested in these experiences. He has interviewed over 100 people who have "returned from the dead" and finds great similarities in many of their stories.

For one thing, the people didn't *feel* "dead" —even though the doctors said they were. One man who was so near death that his body was beginning to get cold said:

"I was in an utterly black void [total emptiness]. It is very difficult to explain, but I felt as if I were moving in a vacuum, just through blackness. Yet I was quite conscious. It was like

Numerous people who have *almost* died have told their stories to Dr. Raymond Moody, Jr., author of "Life After Life."

being in a cylinder which had no air in it. It was a feeling of limbo, of being halfway here and halfway somewhere else."

While they were in the black emptiness of near-death, many of Dr. Moody's subjects also reported *meeting other people!* Sometimes these spiritual beings talked to them, telling them not to be afraid of passing from life to death. In other cases, the spirits told them it was not their time to die. Their souls must return to their bodies and resume their lives in the real world.

Most important, people who experience "life after life," as Moody calls it, lose their fear of death. Says Moody, "They have seen death and know that it is even more than life was. It is a continuing cycle, not an abrupt end."

Reincarnation then, although it has not yet been proven, does present some interesting paths for our minds to explore. Do you find it strange? Does the thought that you might have lived in the time of the Egyptians or in the time of Marie Antoinette strike you as frightening? Or is it comforting to know that there may be a life after life?

MYSTERIES YET UNSOLVED

No matter how incredible the idea of reincarnation seems, it's hard to ignore the thousands of stories, experiments, and dreams of other-life experiences. Could all those people have just *imagined* past lives? Many details about these other lives could only be known by them if they had *really* experienced them. No books could have provided the memories.

Some people remember the day they died in other lives. They have described how they felt and what caused them to die. Like Moody's "life after life" cases, none of them expressed any sense of fear or terror about the experience.

Many describe happy scenes from previous lives—getting married, receiving a new toy, or going to a party. They also give reports of how they looked in those previous times. One tall, dark-haired, and beautiful woman, while under hypnosis, described herself in another life as having been a "little, blue-eyed, blonde boy." Other people have even described their own birth scene. One woman was able to recall the doctor handing her to her father a few minutes after she was born.

Another woman remembered the day she was brought home from the hospital: "More clearly than anything is my memory of observing my mother and wondering, Who is she? What am I? And who are those people standing on the porch? Since I was a young child, I have always had the feeling of total detachment from myself and others, as if I were on the outside looking in."

Studies have shown that children seem to have an easier time than adults recalling events from past lives. Maybe it's because the young mind is less crowded with details of everyday life.

Children also make good subjects because they could not possibly have known the details of the lives they report. Sometimes they report long ago events and places in history. Other times they speak in foreign languages or have heavy accents.

Hans Holzer, a leading expert on reincarnation, tells the case of Brenda H., a young child in Montana. Suddenly, one Good Friday morning, little Brenda awoke from a sound sleep and started to talk about a previous life. She described living in a big house in the old South be-

Brenda described the old Southern mansion in which she had lived.

fore the Civil War. When asked if there were other children, Brenda said there were a lot of slave children. Brenda hadn't even studied history yet. She knew nothing of slavery in the South. Even more amazing, this little American girl gave a French name and spoke with a heavy French accent!

Holzer, who has written many books about reincarnation, also reports the baffling case of Ellen S., a ten-year-old girl. She had been troubled by recurring dreams about another young girl when Holzer saw her. Even though they didn't look alike, Ellen thought that she was actually the other girl in her dreams.

In the dream, one scene kept repeating itself. The girl was riding a horse. When the horse jumped over a fence, a terrible accident happened. The rider and the horse fell. And the little girl died.

Ellen's dream was so clear she could see that the girl was living in the late 1800s. Finally, one night Ellen dreamed a further clue to the mysterious girl's identity. Still asleep, Ellen sat up in bed and started talking. She said: "Clara J. Wiston, Clara J. Wiston is coming for me."

Was Ellen once Clara J. Wiston? Had she been the one to die in a riding accident? If so, who was Clara and what was she like?

In Ellen's dream, the little girl fell from her horse as he jumped a fence.

Hans Holzer checked the girl's story in every way he could. Eventually, he found out that a Wiston family had lived in New England in 1665. Was Clara Wiston a part of that family?

Holzer's search is still going on. So, too, is the search for the truth about reincarnation. Are we born today because we were born yesterday? The idea is very mysterious—and someday we just may find the answer.